MOTIF MEDLEY
adult coloring book for relaxation
Volume 1

by Ifraj Suad

In this book you will find a variety of unique hand-drawn illustrations. The title of each art piece is located on the back of the page. Use colored pencils, crayons or markers to color the designs any way you like. When coloring, place a blank sheet between the pages to help prevent bleed-through. Discover your inner artist and frame your creations for inspiration! I am so excited to share my love for coloring with you. Let your imagination soar and fall in love too!

-Ifraj Suad

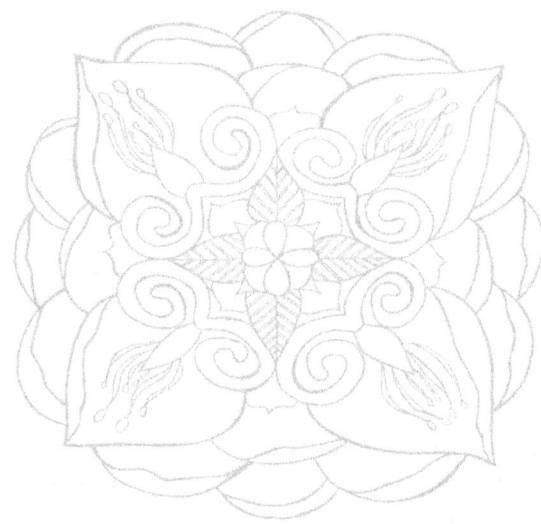

Follow us and share your colored pages:

Instagram.com/ colorwithifraj
www.colorwithifraj.com
Email/ info@ifrajsuad.com

*In honour of my father E.Lutfee,
a true artist.*

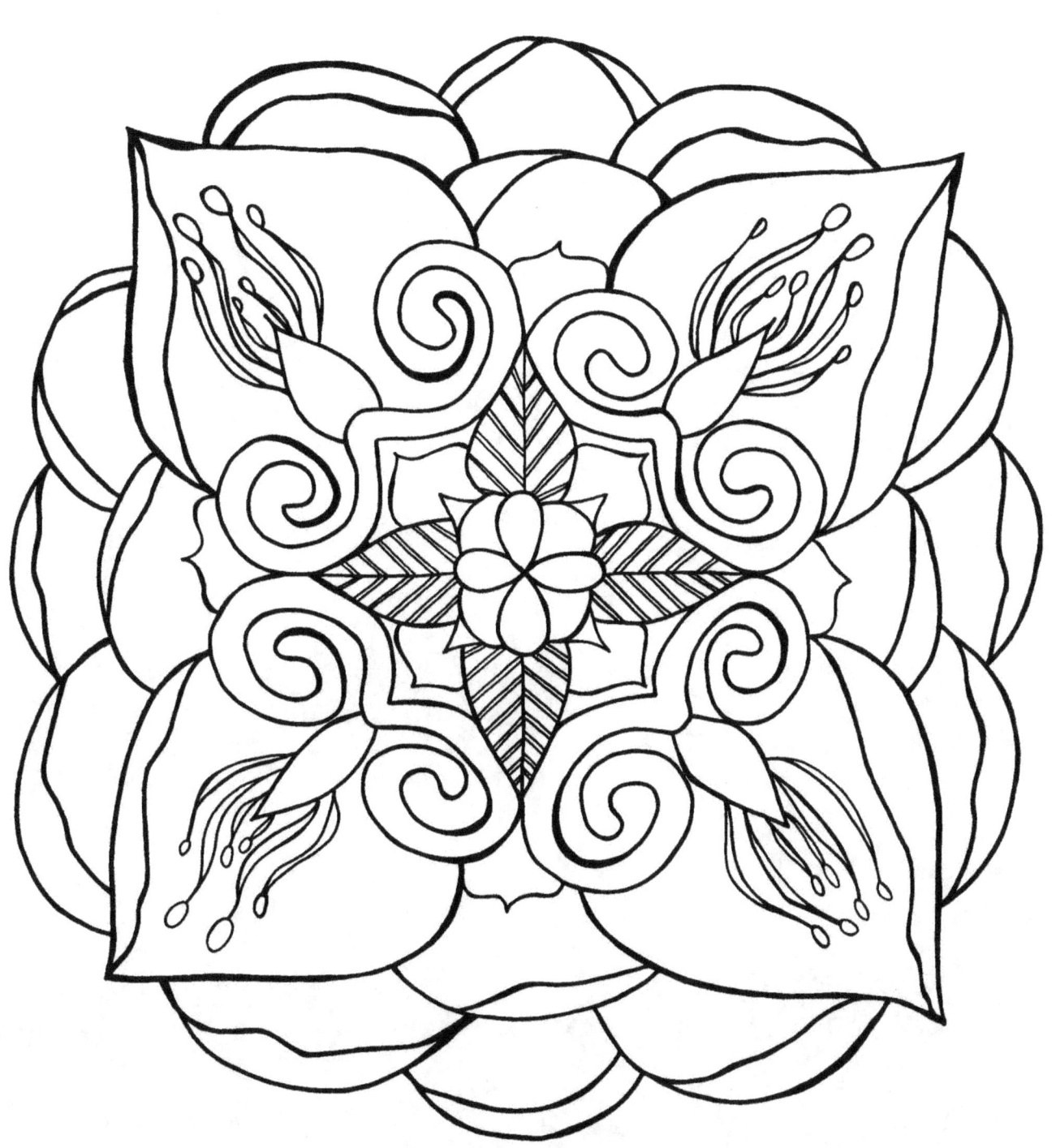

1 - "Blossom"

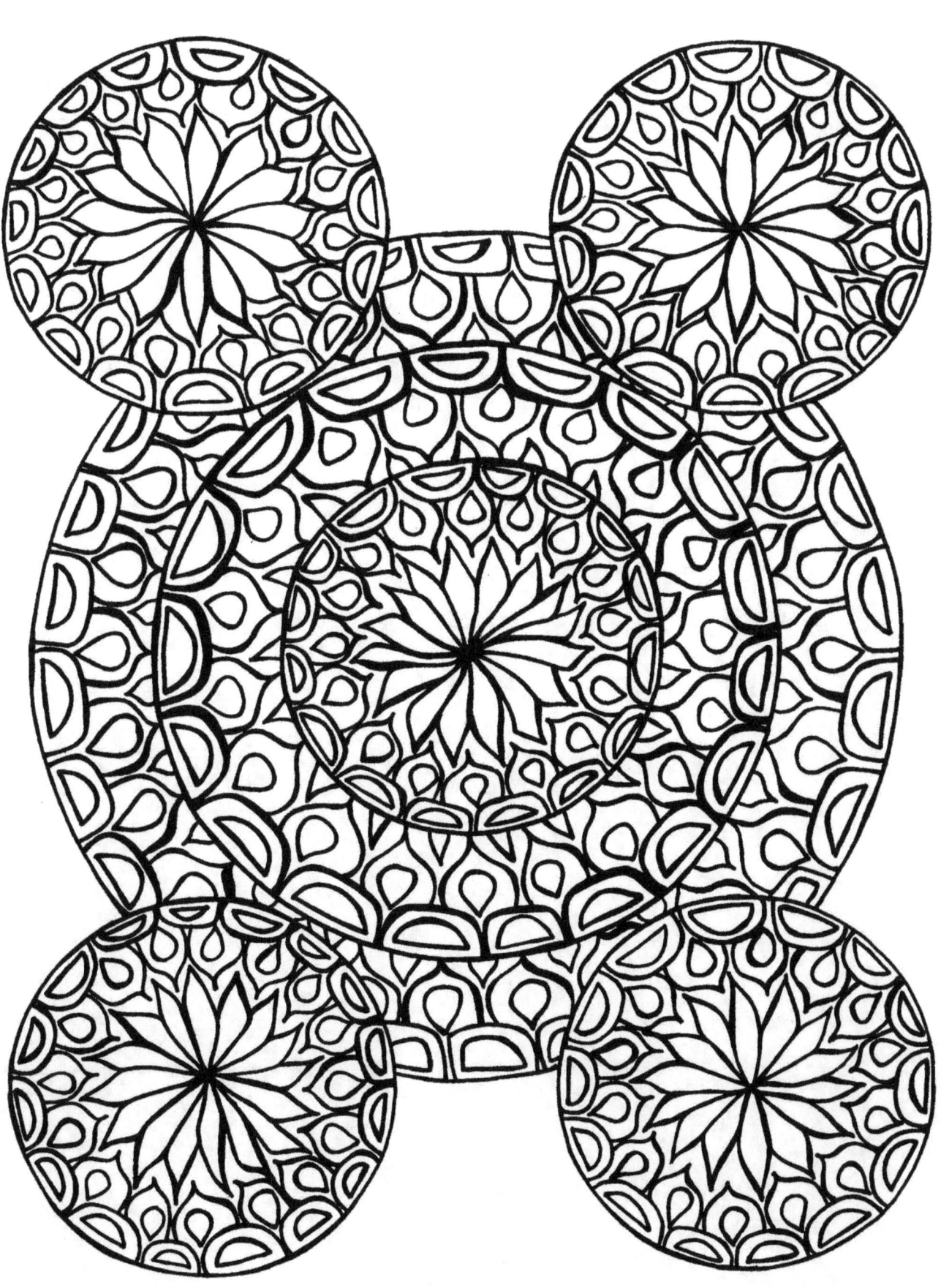

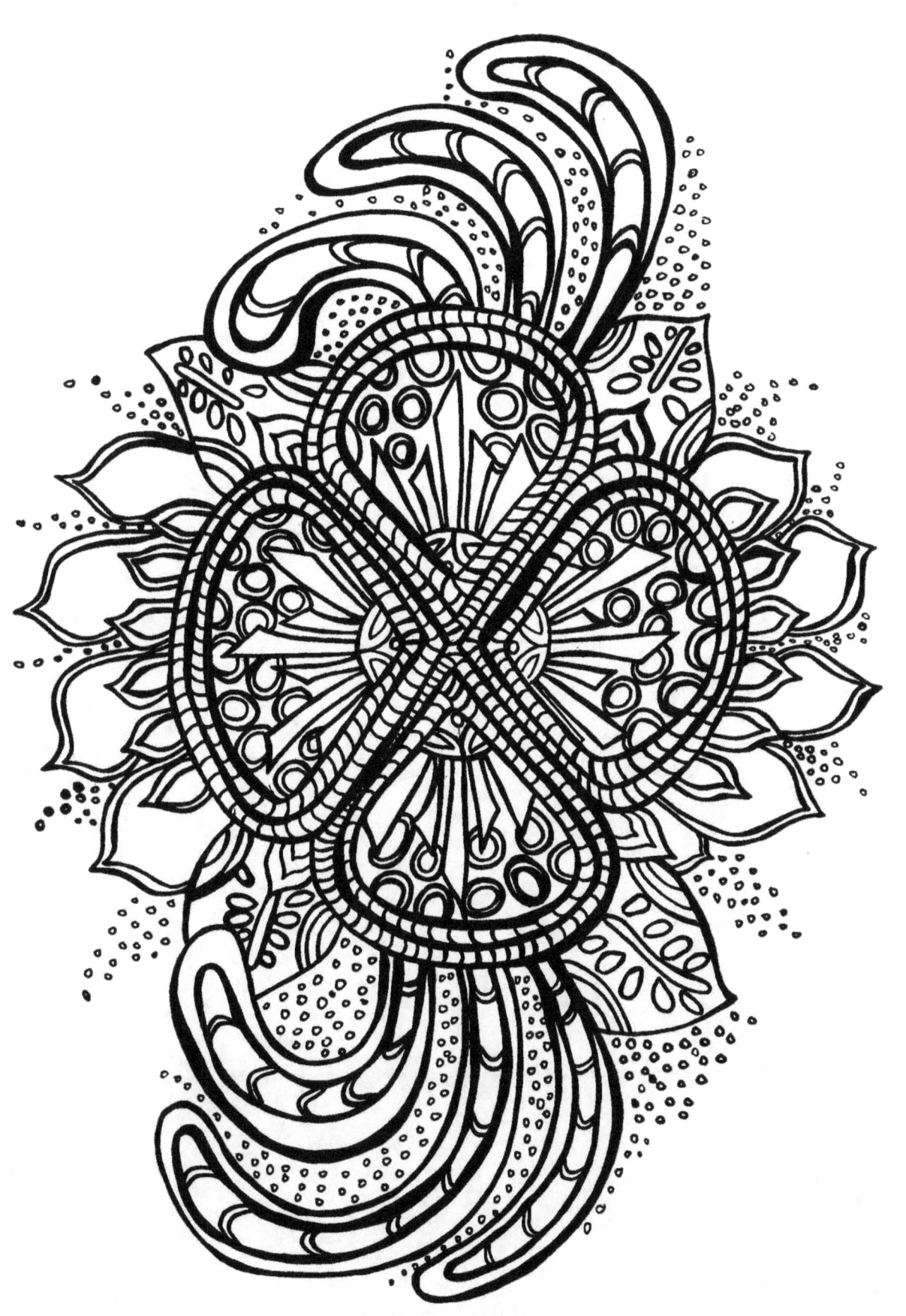

3 - "Underworld"

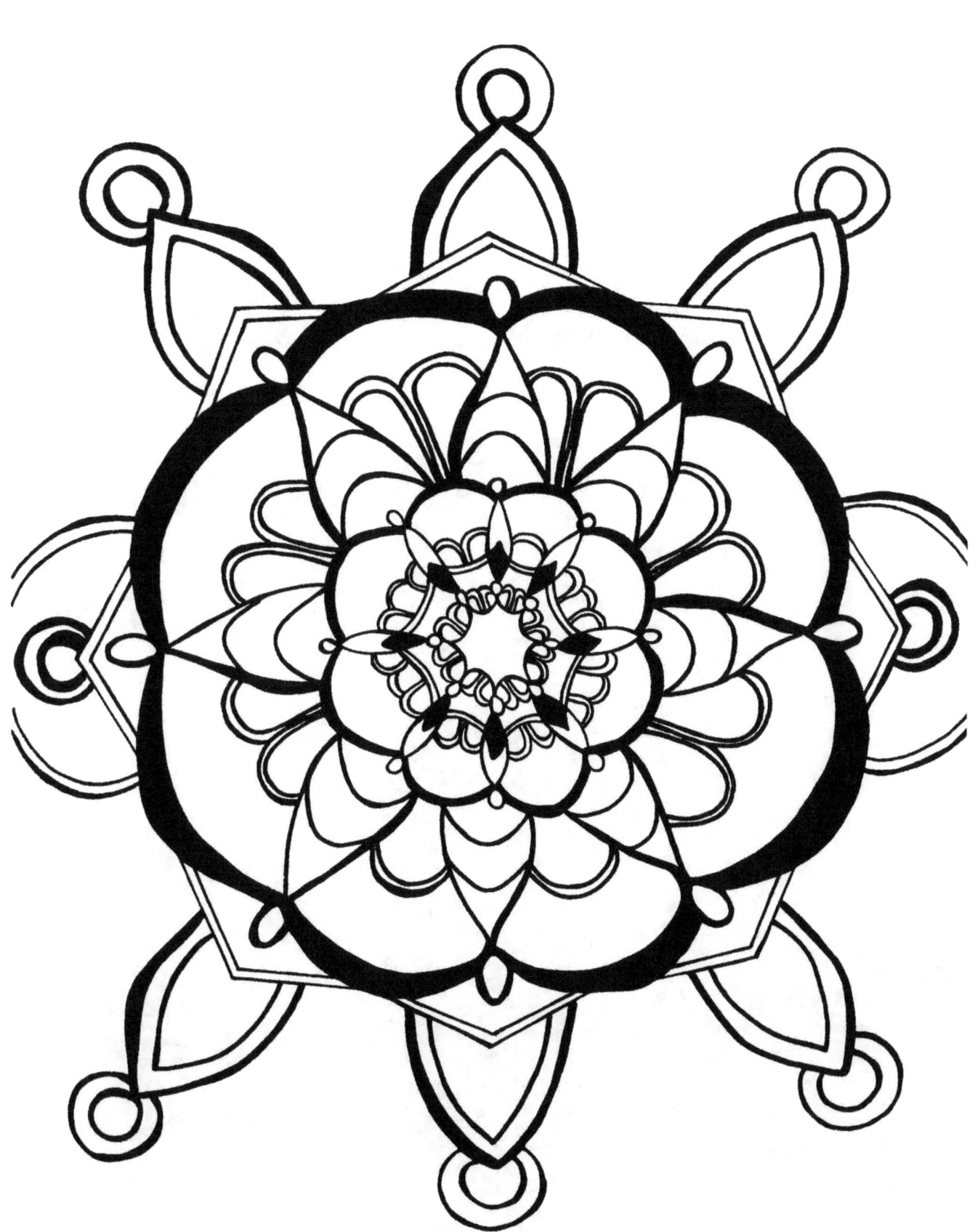

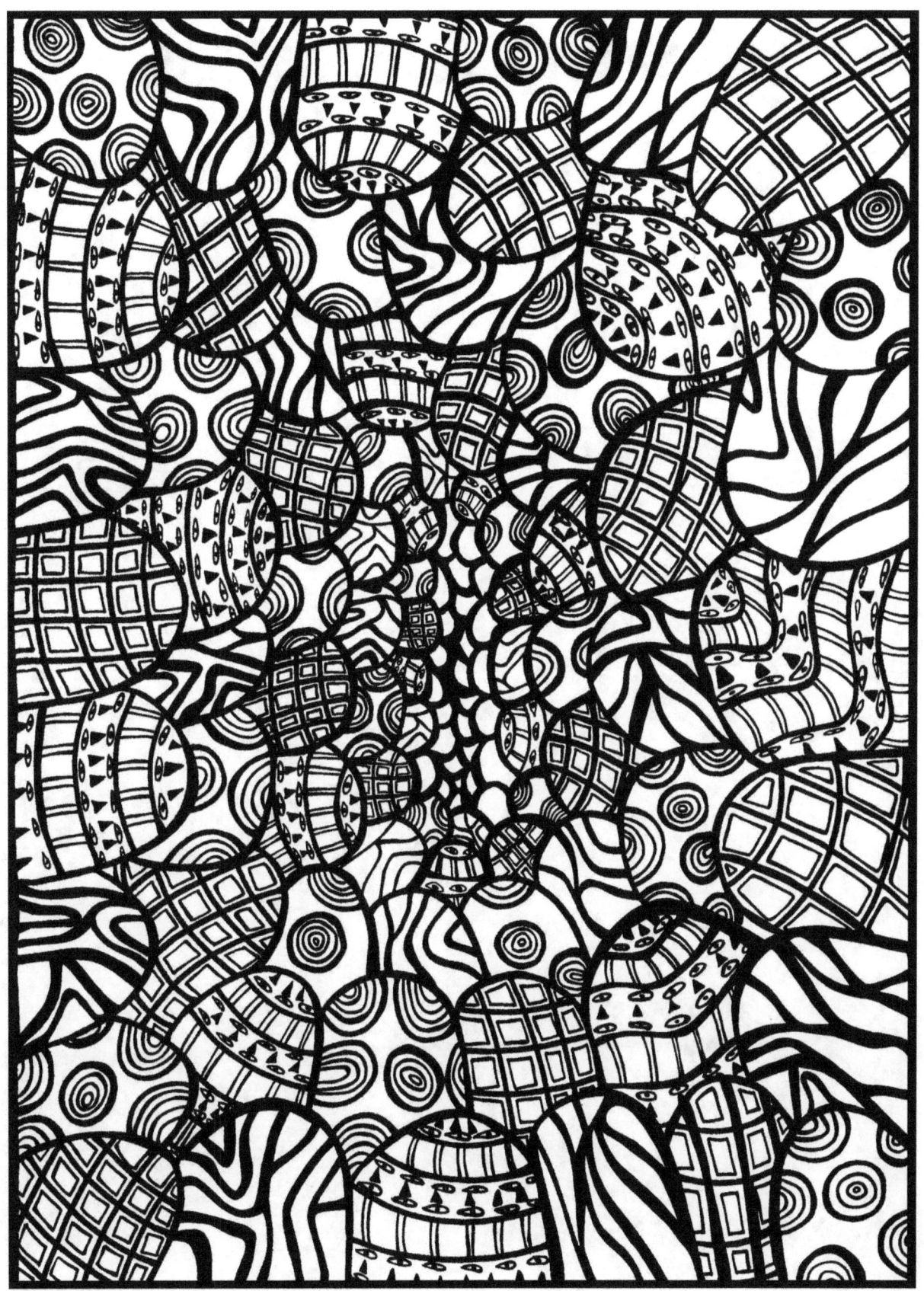

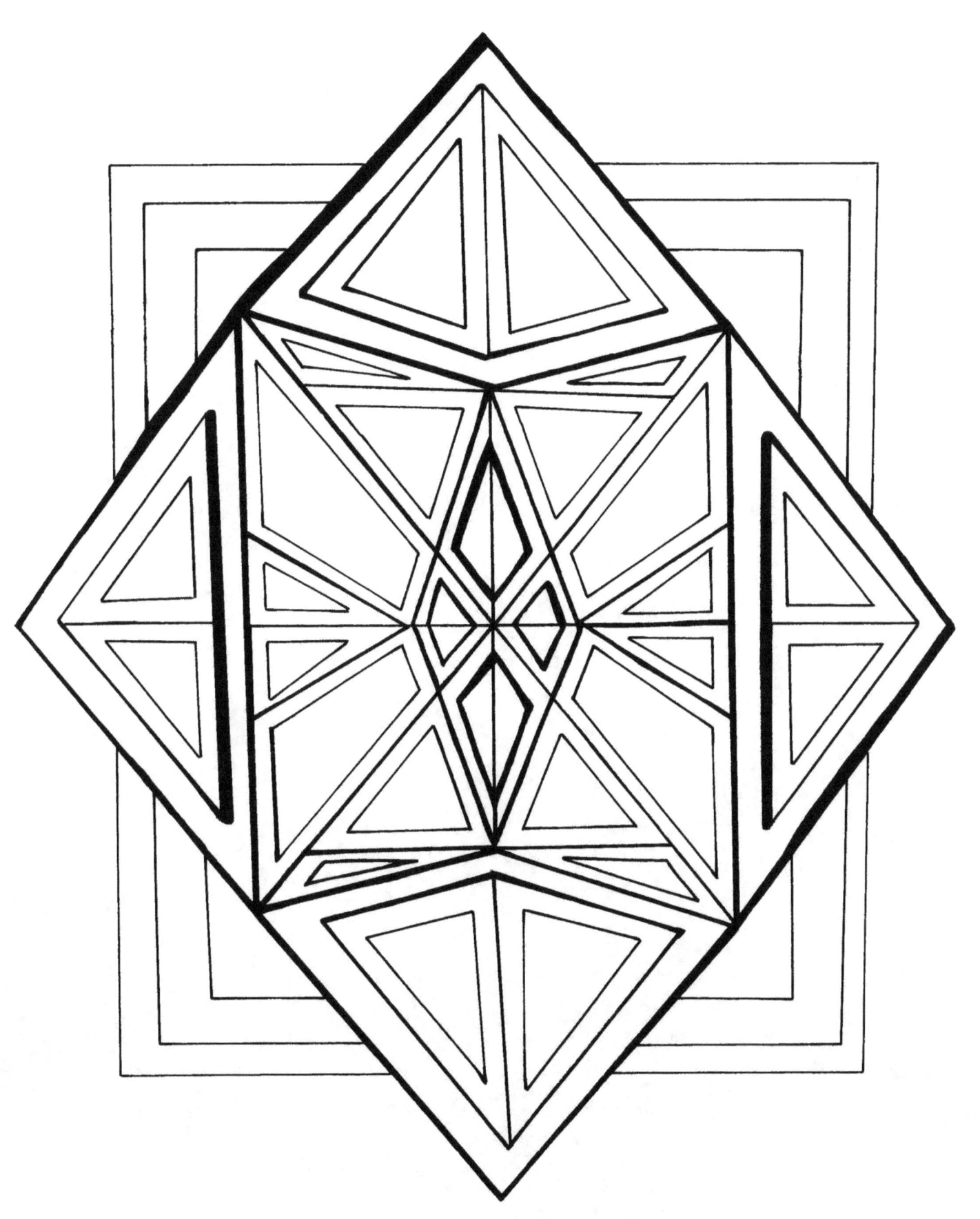

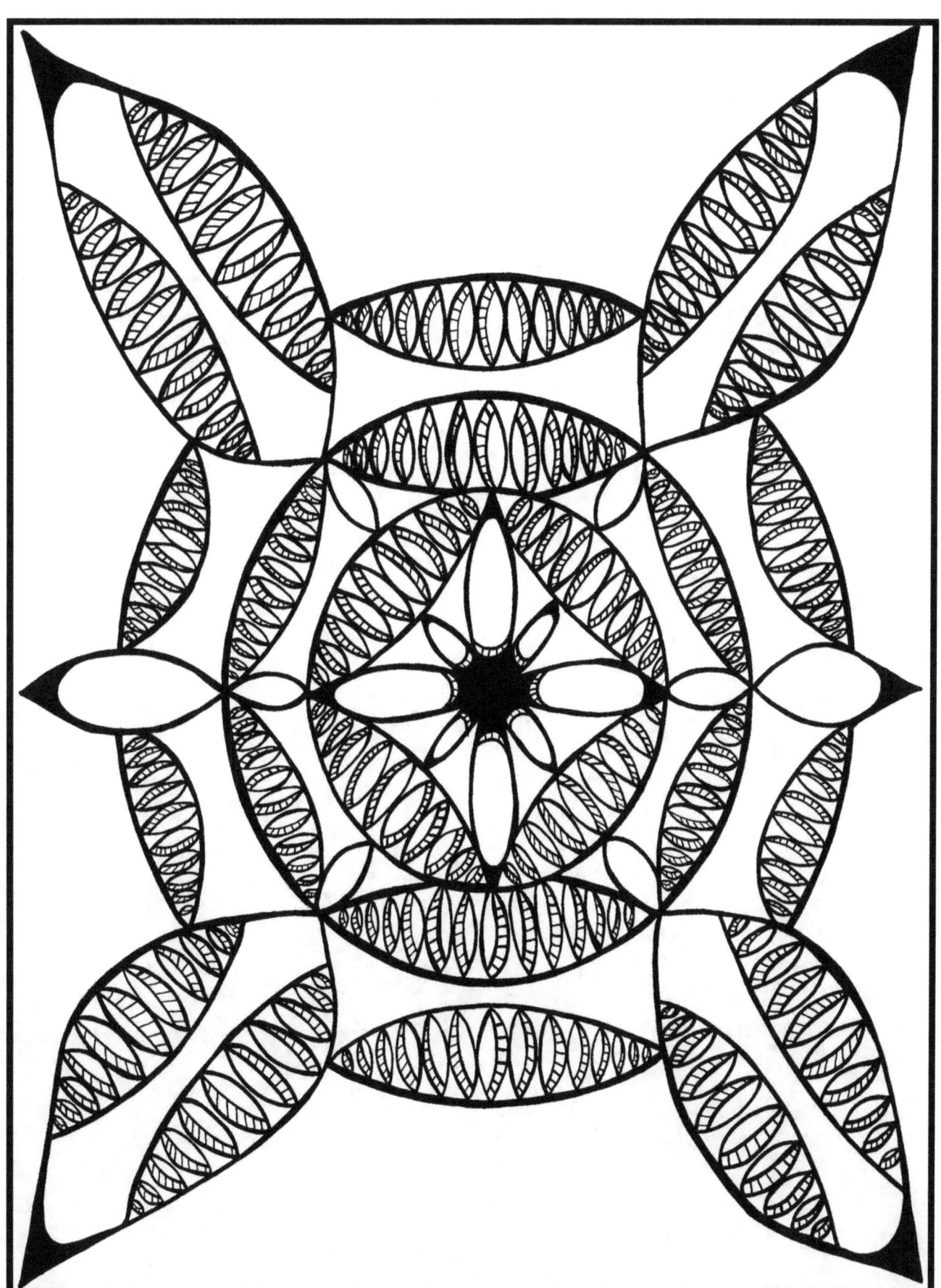

7 - "Wired"

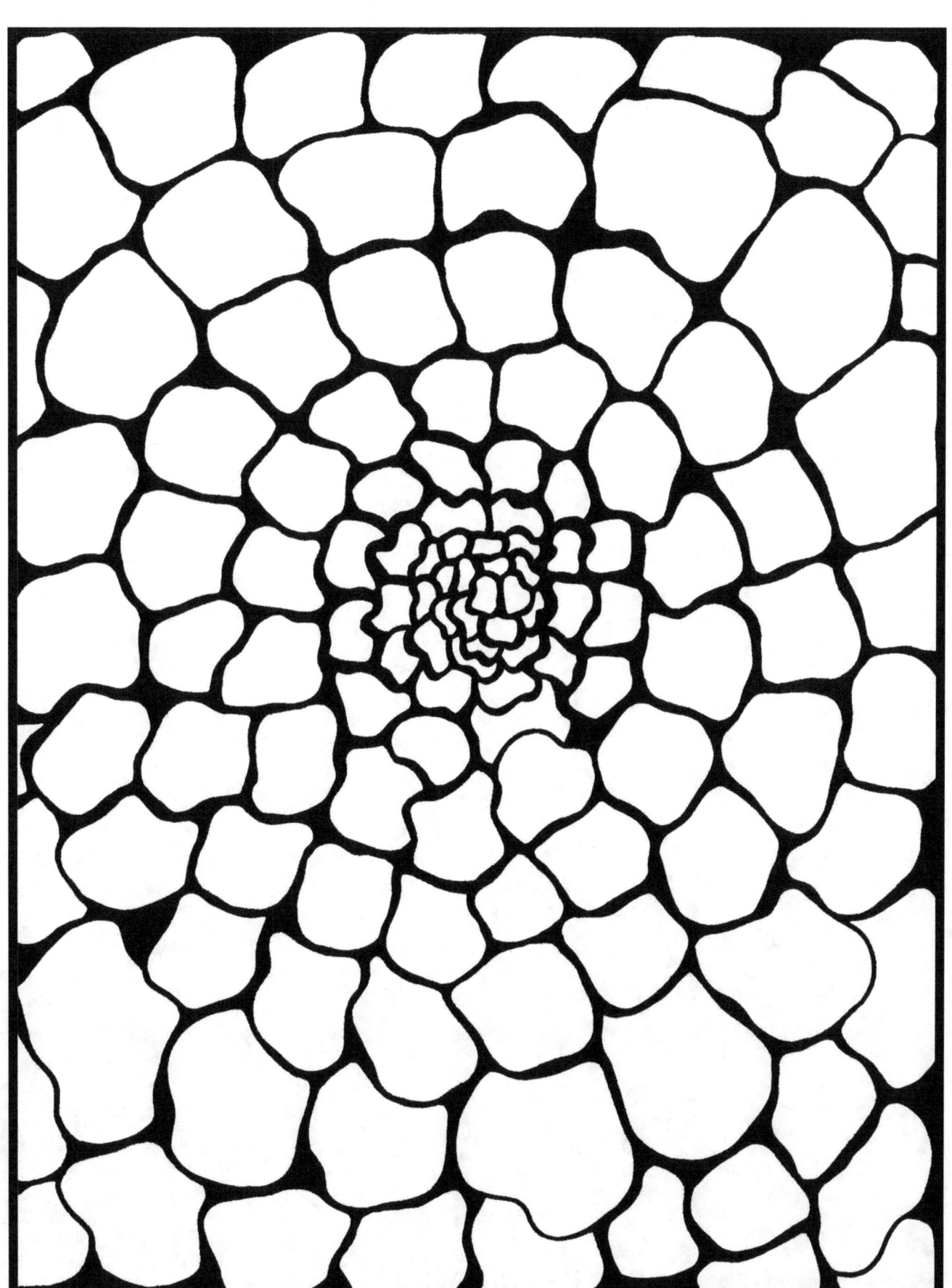

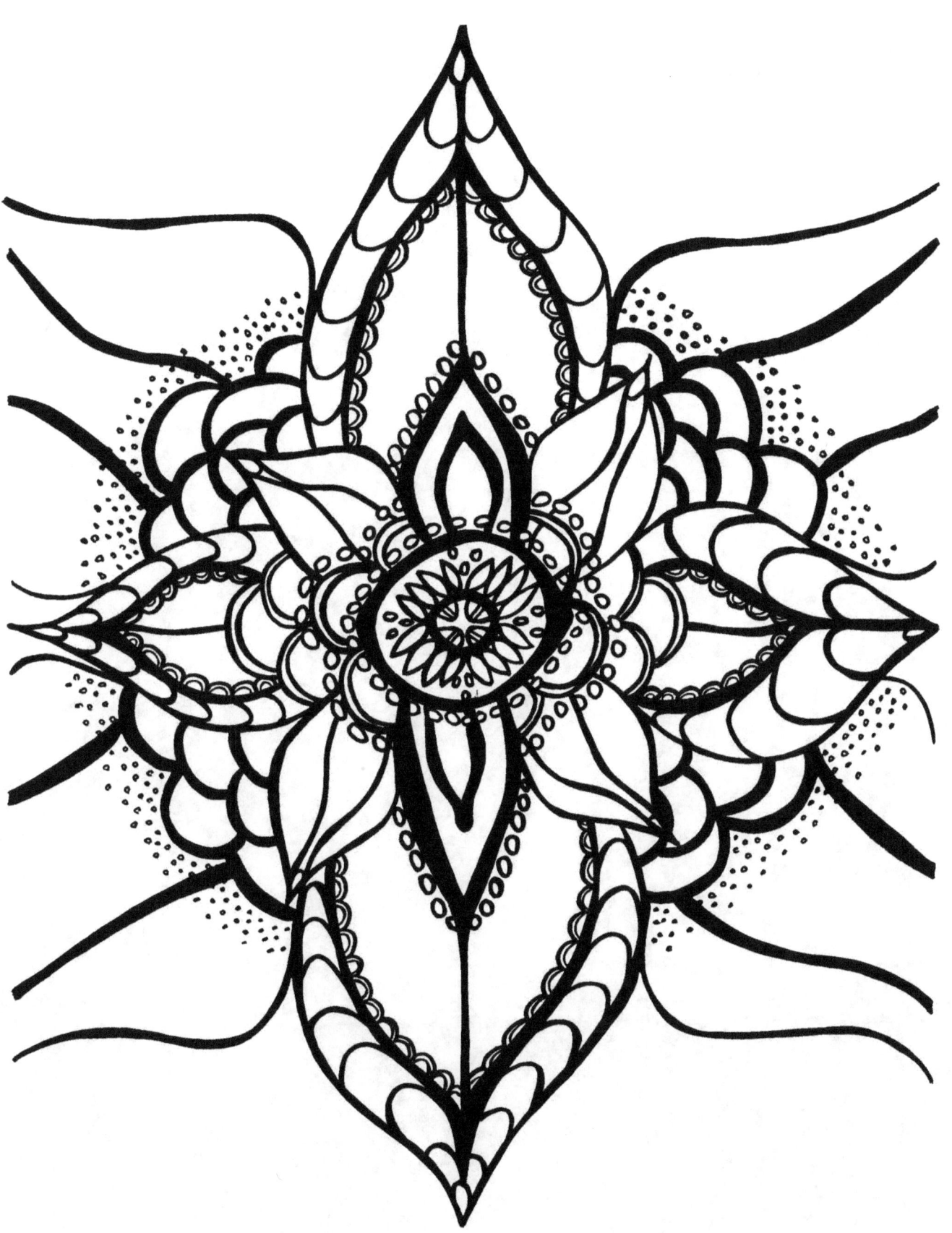

9 - "Mother Earth"

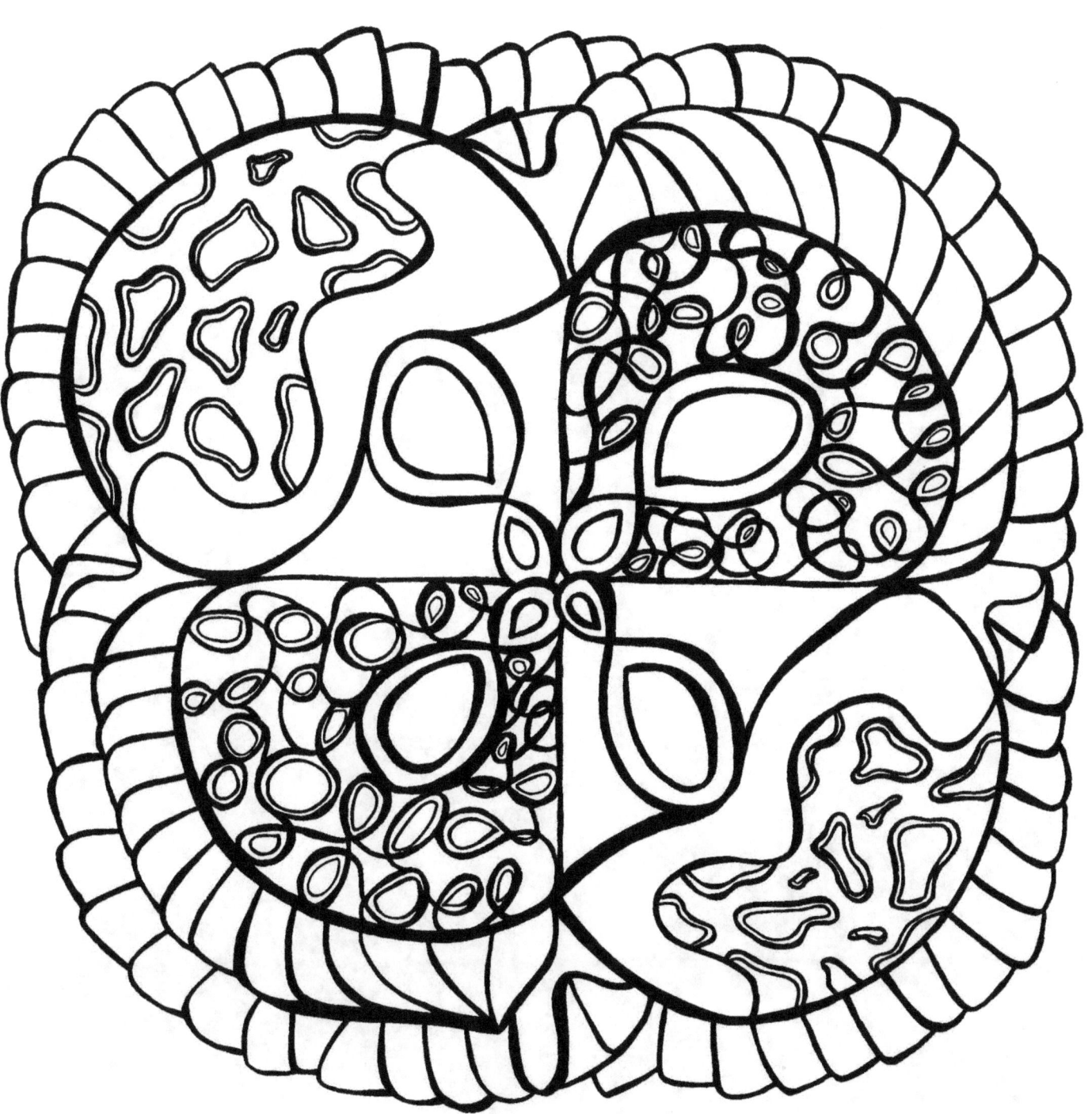

10 - "Party City"

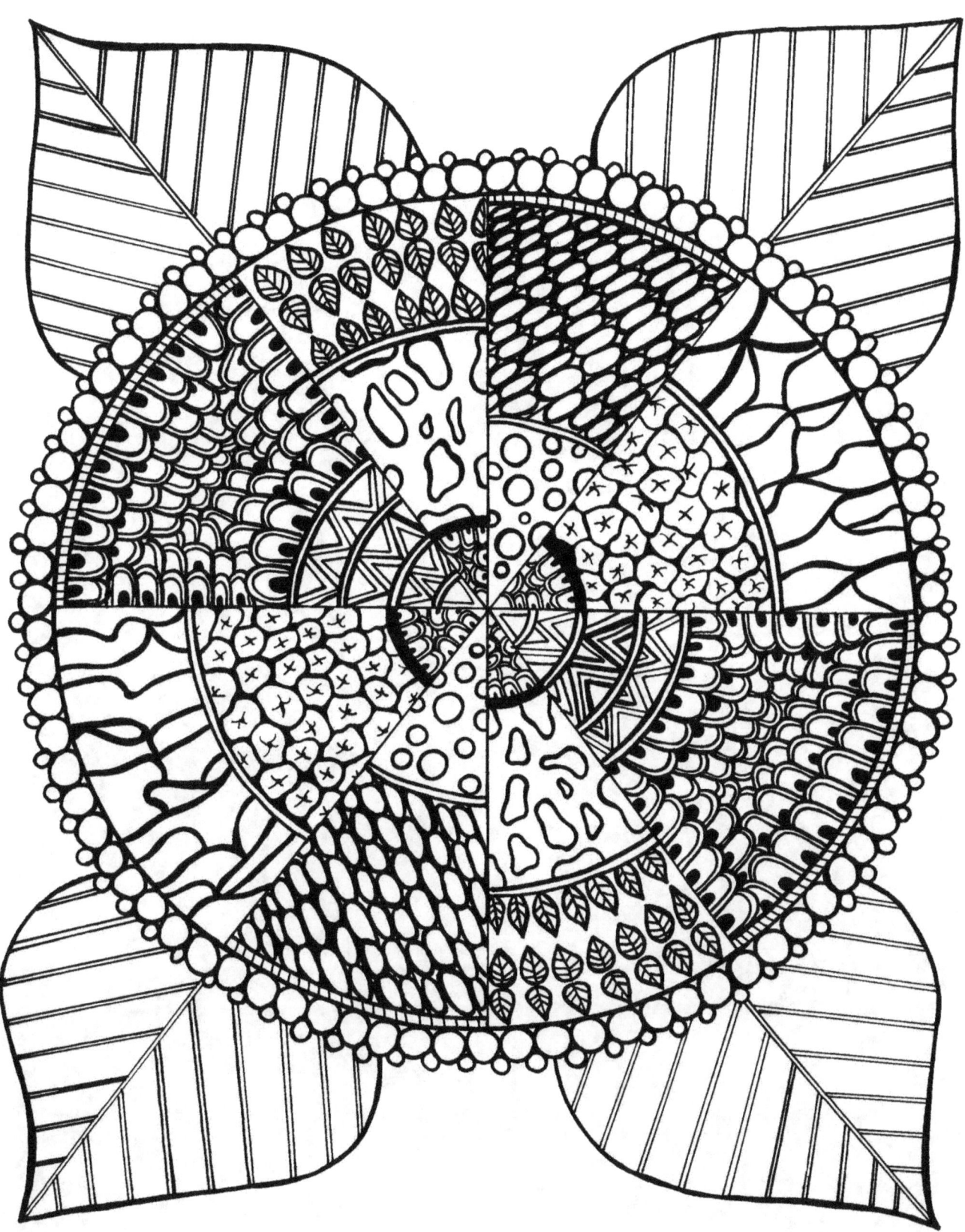

11 - "Peace of Me"

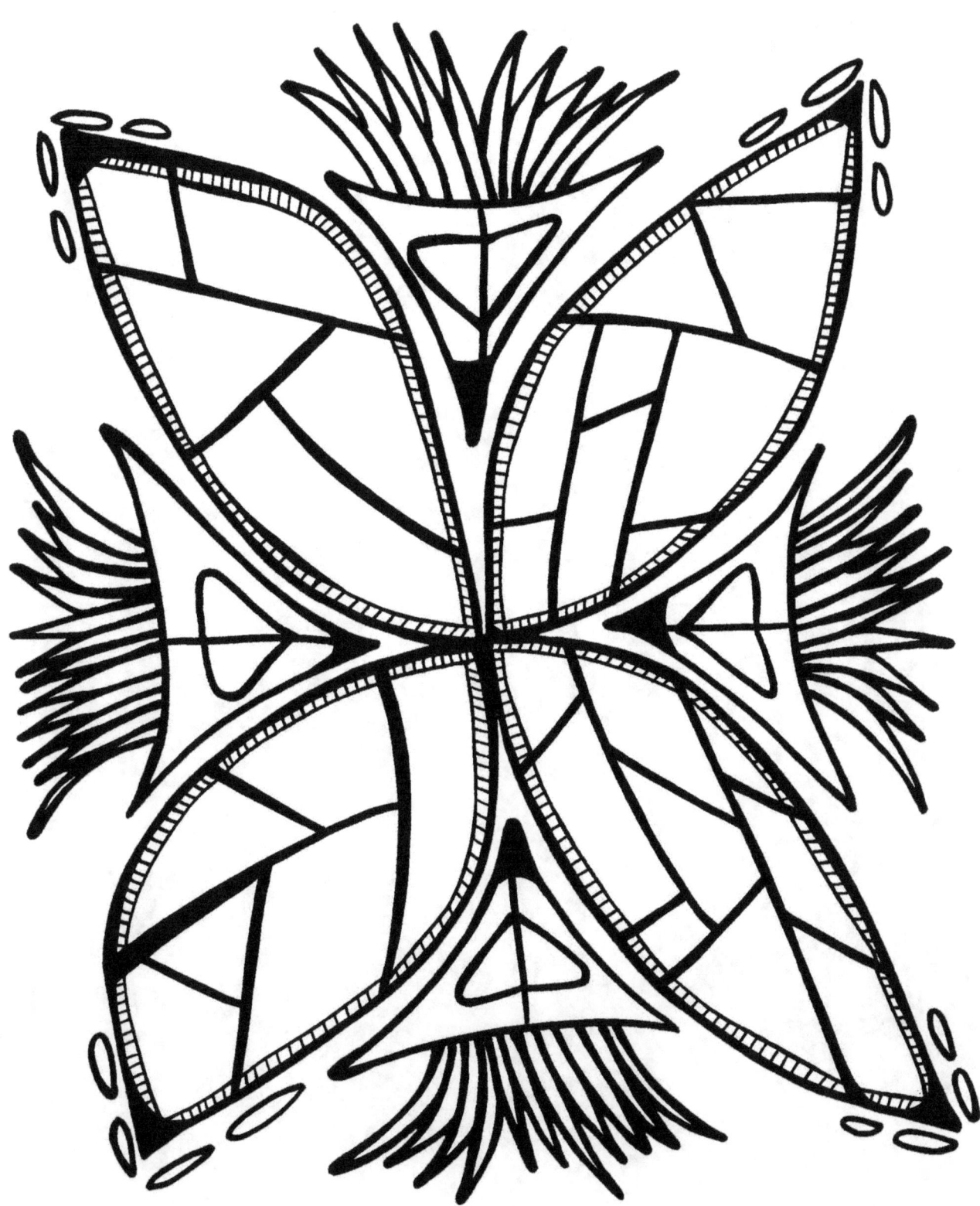

12 - "Dance"

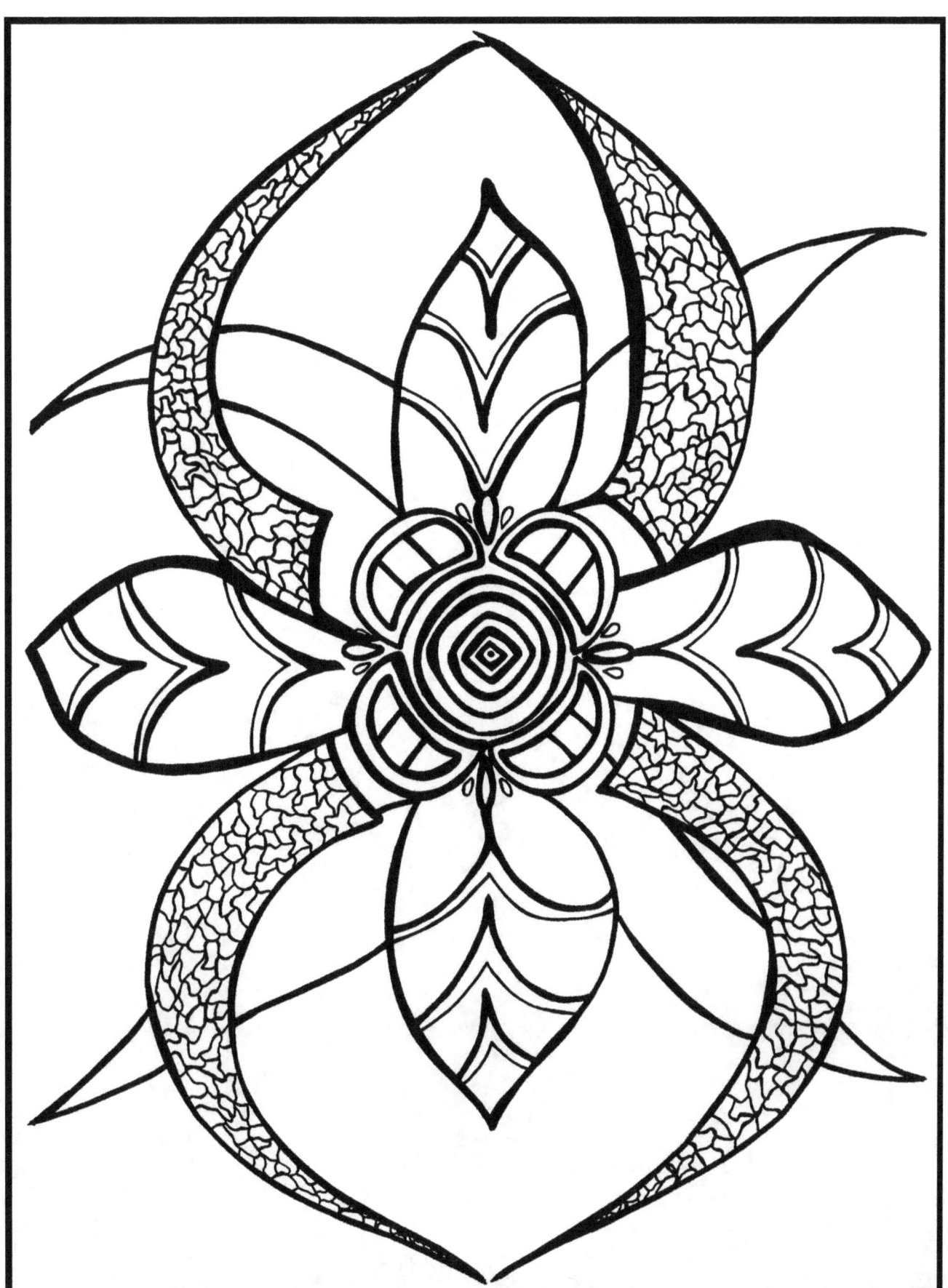

13 - "Charlotte"

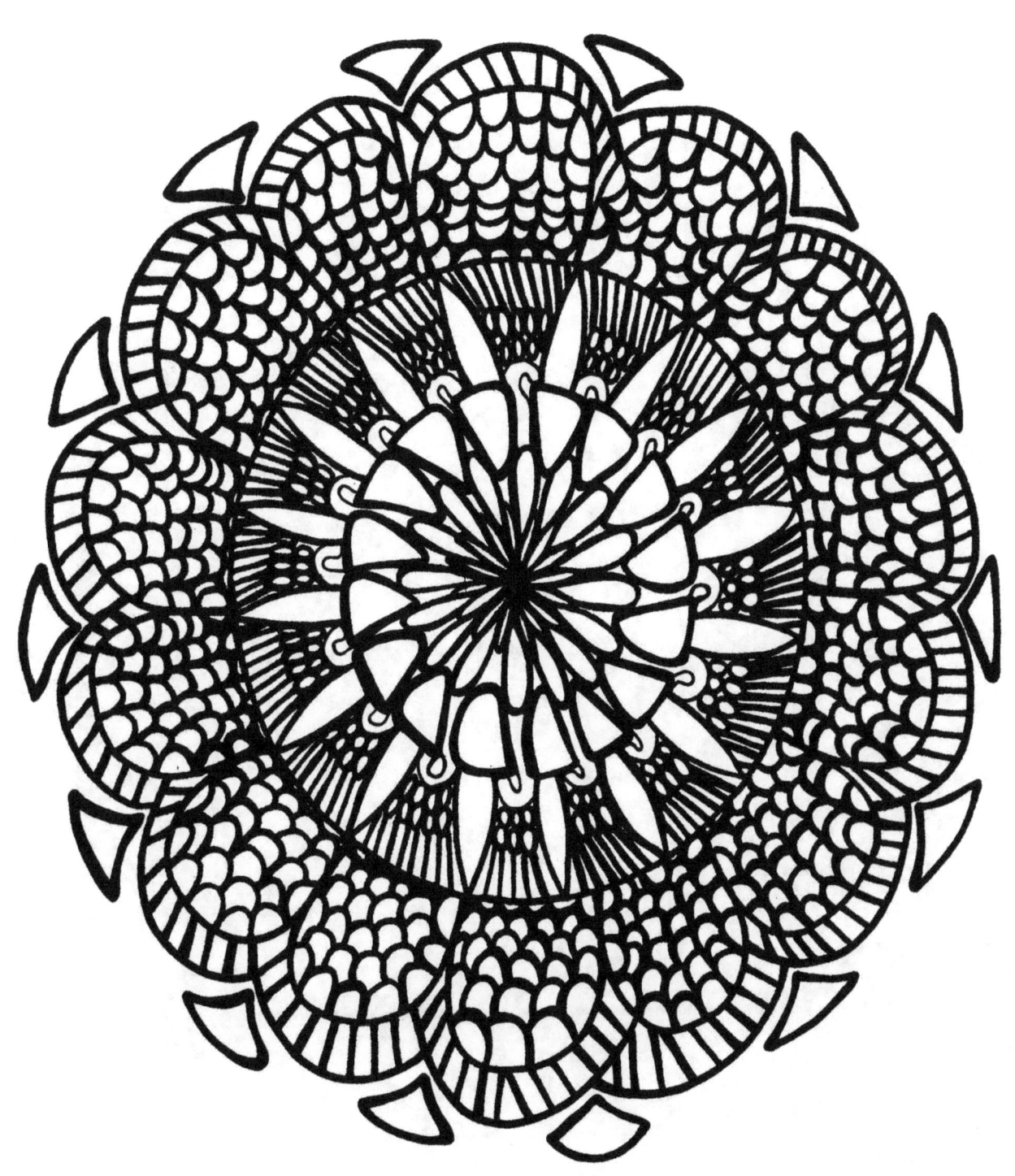

14 - "Blood Orange"

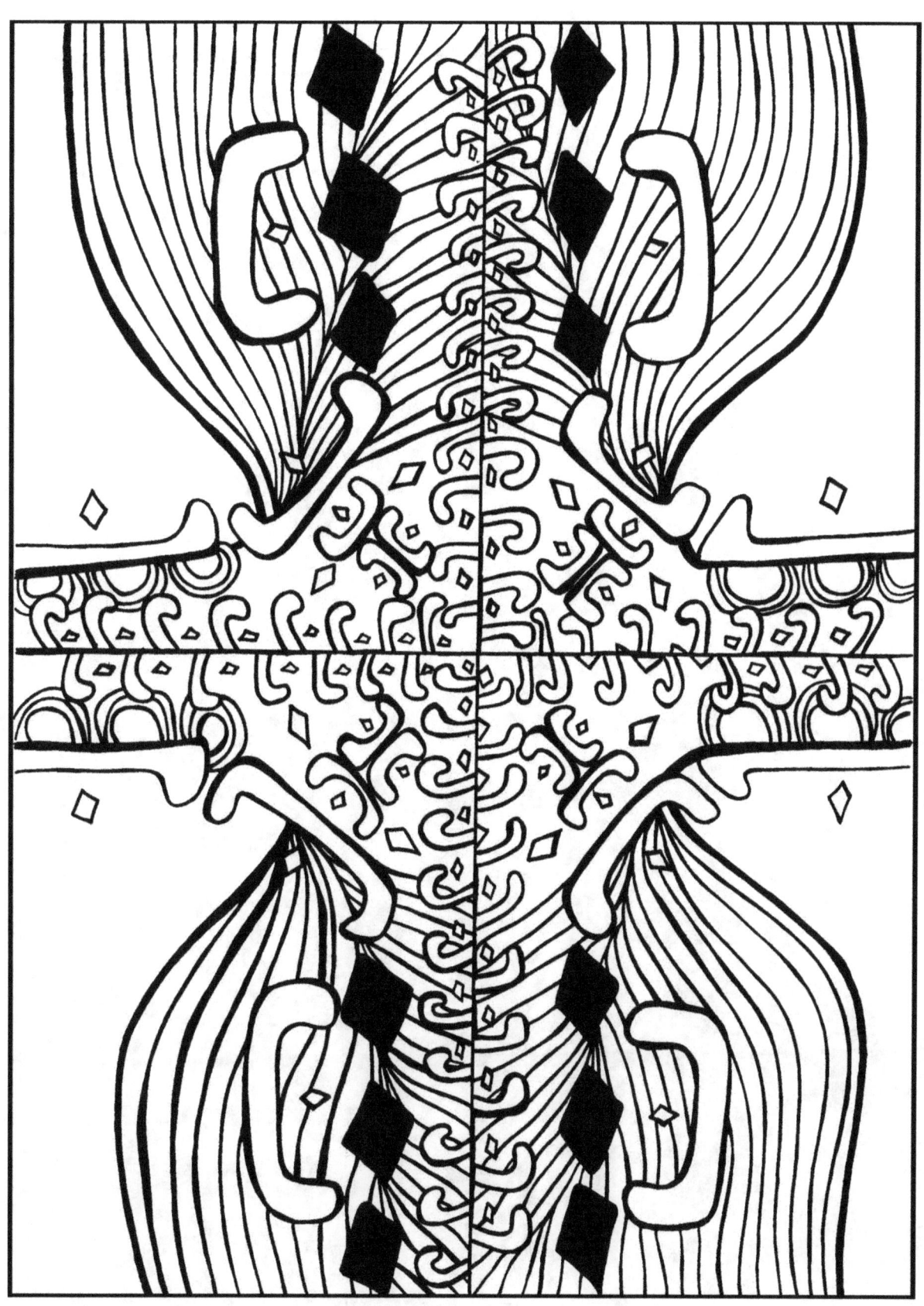

15 - "Transform"

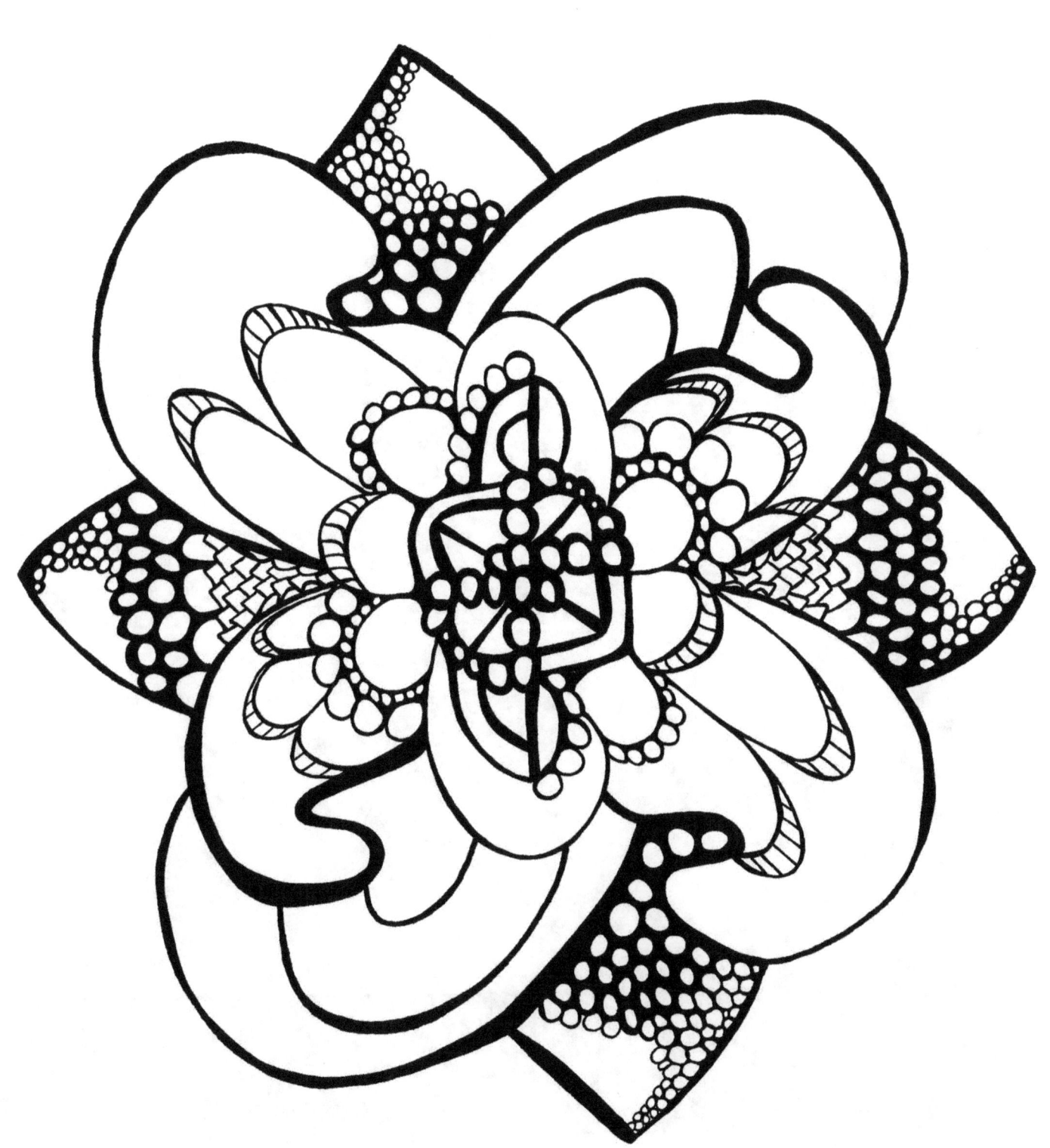

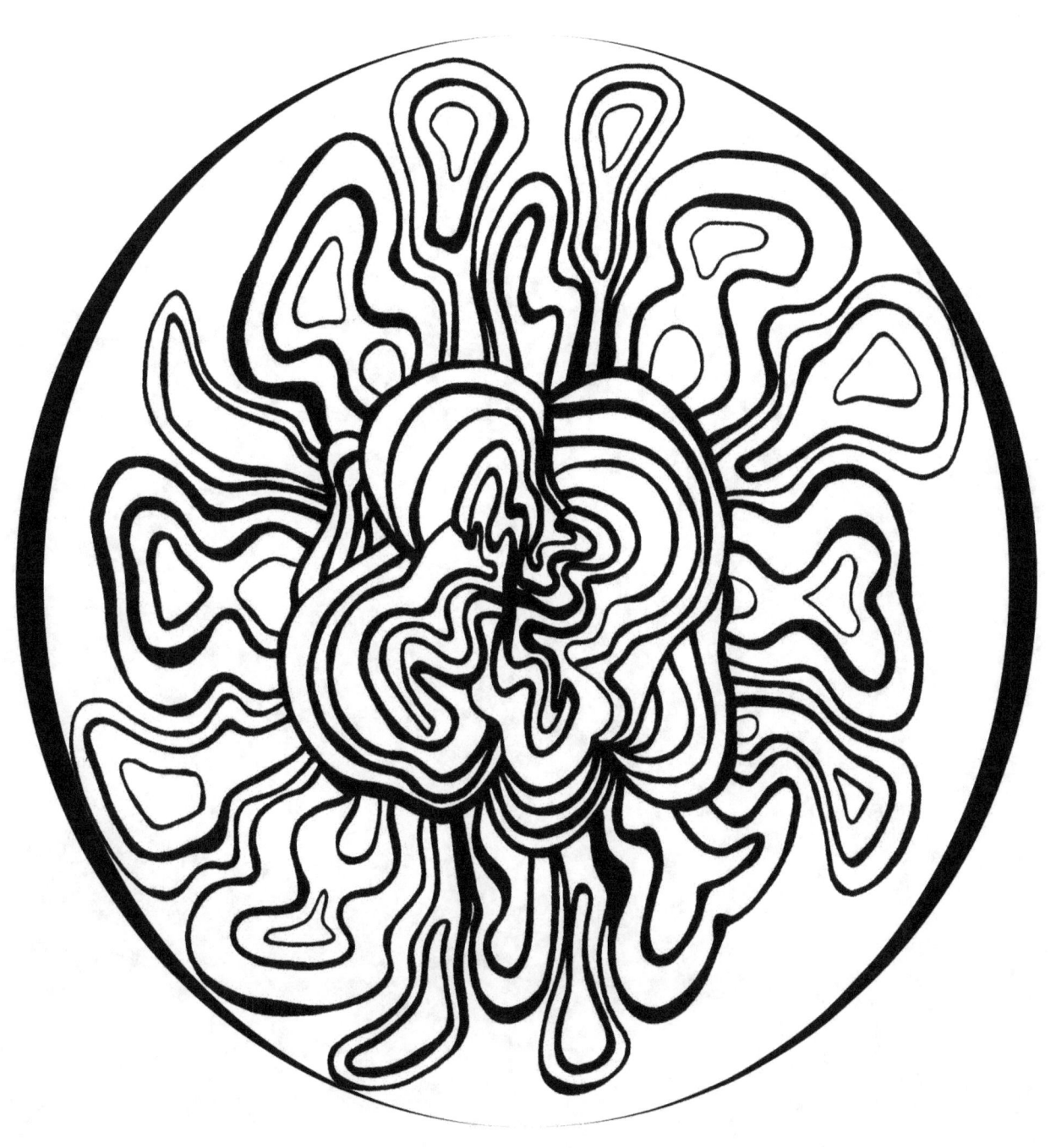

17 - "Perfectly Imperfect"

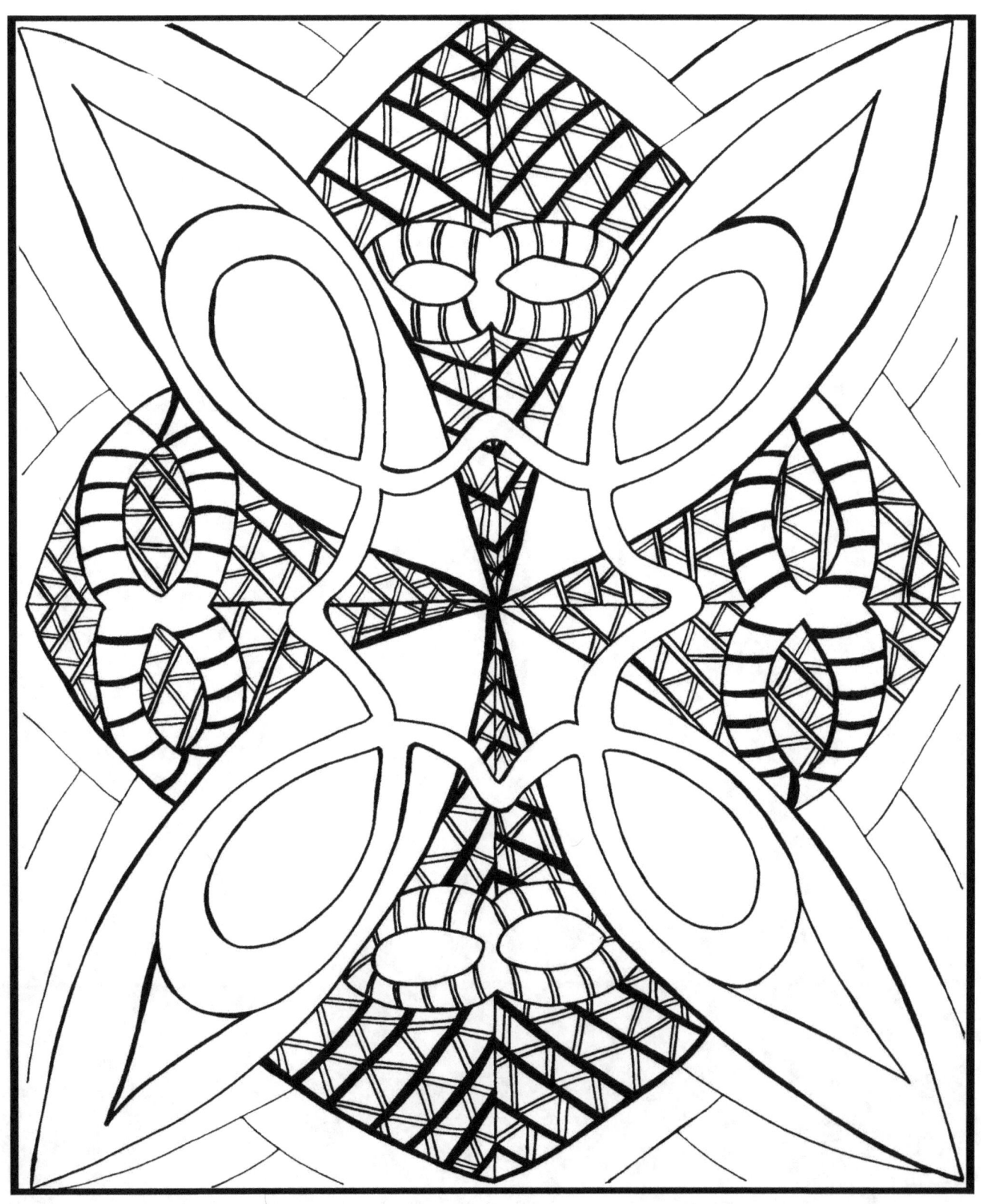

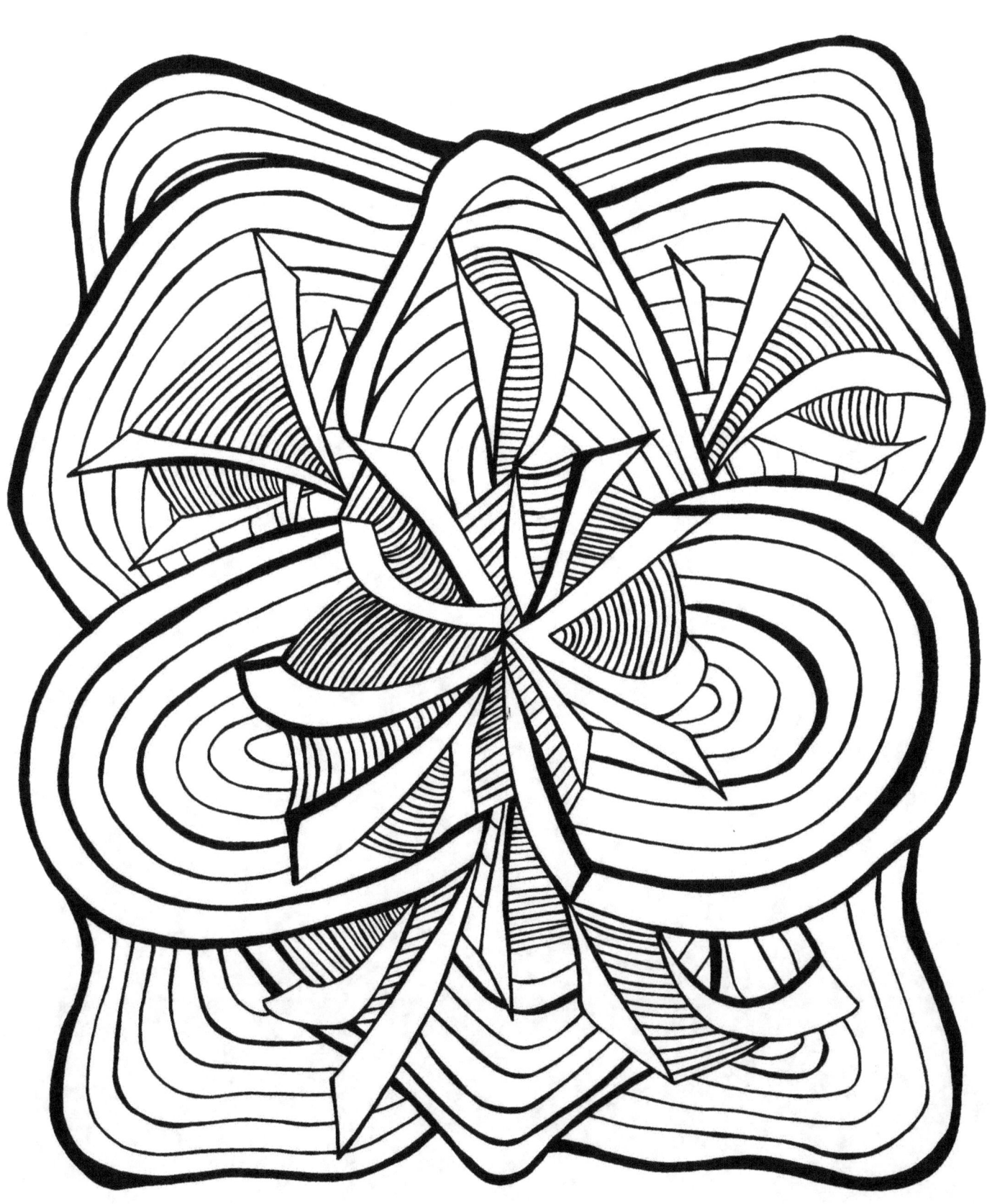

19 - "Lost"

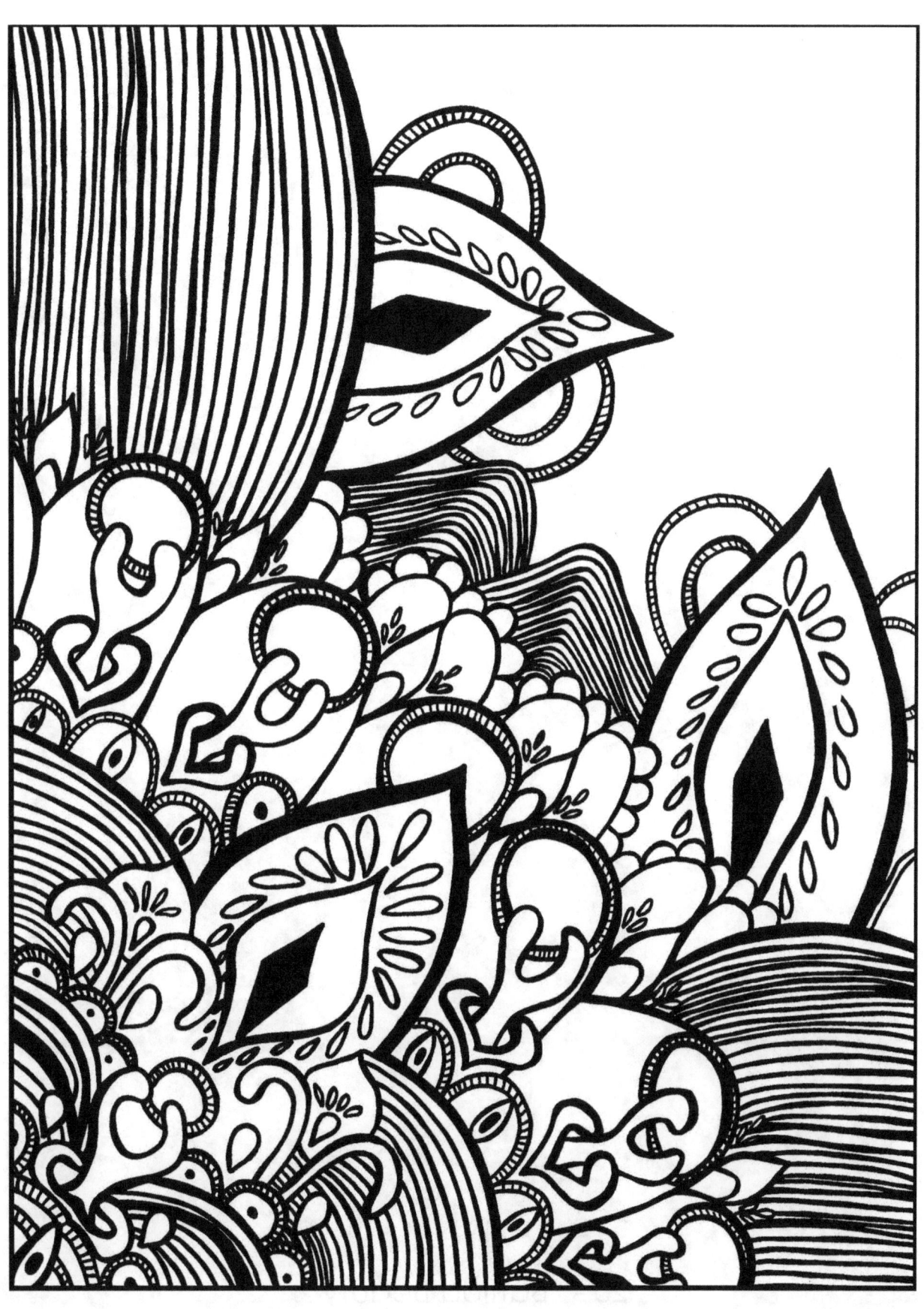

www.ingramcontent.com/pod-product-compliance
Lightning Source LLC